TASTE OF MIAMI

A COVID-19 RELIEF EFFORT FOR THE RESTAURANTS WE LOVE

100% of all sales go back to
the bussers, servers, dishwashers, and cooks
that need it most.

Querido Miami,

Miami's diverse culinary scene is one of the richest cultural mixes in the world. Our gastronomy keeps getting better, giving us the opportunity to try food from almost anywhere in the world, right here in our backyard.

But when the pandemic hit, the food scene took a notable hit. Some of our iconic and favorite places to eat couldn't withstand the shutdown, and since then have closed. When I heard what neuelane was doing to give back to local restaurants, I felt I needed to be a part of it. I love Miami and donating my time for recipe testing was the least I could do to get this project off the ground.

I encourage everyone to buy this cookbook; not just for themselves, but for family and friends. Know that with each purchase, you are helping the employees that work in the restaurants featured in this book. I also encourage you to share any social media posts you see about this book, because the more people know about it, the better.

This book has captured an array of recipes from the Miami we know and love, and with that I give you a Taste of Miami.

Buen provecho!

Jesus 'Chef Yisus' Diaz

FOREWORD

Sef Gonzalez
Burger Beast

If you told me back when I wrote my first blog post in 2008 that Miami would have become a home to such phenomenal cuisine, I might not have believed it.

Back then, our city was overflowing with many average chains that folks were accepting as good. The interest in food television seemed to open up many local foodies' eyes to what cuisine was out there waiting for them.

Once Edible South Florida appeared, it was a sign that things were changing in our local food world for the better. Chefs like Eileen Andrade, Jose Mendin, Ralph Pagano, Giorgio Rapicavoli, Cesar Zapata, and the legendary Allen Susser continue to excite locals with their cuisine. I'm happy that some of their recipes have found their way into Taste of Miami.

Before I go any further, I need to give a shoutout to neuelane for what feels like the sometimes thankless job of creating and coordinating this massive enterprise, the Taste of Miami book. 100% of the profits will go towards the eateries and their staff affected by Covid-19.

The pandemic has hit everyone hard, but our restaurant families have suffered financially the most. Your purchase of this book means you want to help; it means you want to see more sacks of flour turn into a béchamel sauce and, eventually, a delicious Miami-style croqueta. You know that a croqueta reference had to make an appearance sooner or later.

Speaking of croquetas, you can now make Kush by Stephen's Reuben, Doce Provisions' Chorizo, and Dos Croquetas' Sunday Brunch Croquetas at home. It also means you can invite your friends over and be the belle of the ball once you've perfected these local culinary masterpieces.

Another unexpected inclusion is the Arbetter family recipe for Chicken Cacciatore. Yes, Arbetter, as in Arbetter's Hot Dogs, one of Miami's landmark businesses. The Taste of Miami has the recipe for Eating House's Cap'n Crunch Pancakes. It's the dish that launched a thousand copycat brunch dishes.

But we're not done; there's more...if it sounds like an infomercial, it's more of my excitement than anything else. I was happily surprised to see the Spicy Mango Philly Cheesesteak Flatbread from Miami Grill here. Raise of hands, how many folks have savored a cheesesteak from Miami Subs after a late-night club run?

My BEAST-loaf recipe found a place amongst all these culinary comfort food greats. I've only made this version of my meatloaf for close friends and family, so I guess that makes us buds now.

Don't skip out on any desserts like the Pastelitos de Guayaba y Queso from Miami food royalty CAO Bakery and the decadent Coconut Arroz con Leche from Latin American Bakery & Cafe.

Last, and certainly not least by any means, are the cocktails by Gabe Urrutia. Gabe and I have worked together on events before, and his cocktails are always on point. He continues to be the perfect ambassador for Miami-style cocktails.

I hope that this book will make you fall in love with cooking again, while at the same time doing good by supporting chefs, artisan food creators, restaurants, and the employees, the industry's lifeblood.

Don't forget to spread the good word to your friends. Taste of Miami is here, and we, as a community, will all be the better for it.

Take care and stay safe out there.

Your BEAST,
Sef Gonzalez

STOP EAT

AND START EATING SOME MIAMI FAVORITES

ING SHIT

TABLE OF CONTENTS

RAW JUCE
19

DOCE PROVISIONS
21

TRP TASTE
23

HUAHUA'S TAQUERIA
25

THE CAFE AT BOOKS & BOOKS
27

SUVICHE
29

CHEF JOSE MENDIN
31

CONCERNED COOK
33

KUSH BY STEPHEN'S
35

DRUNKEN DRAGON
37

YOLO
39

SUSHI MAKI
41

DOS CROQUETAS
43

SERGIO'S RESTAURANT
47

BURGER BEAST
49

SMOKEY BONES
51

NAKED TACO 53	**EL REY DE LAS FRITAS** 67	**FINKA TABLE & TAP** 83	**HONEYBEE DOUGHNUTS** 101
ARBETTER'S HOT DOGS 55	**PINCHO** 69	**GET REAL** 85	**LATIN AMERICAN BAKERY & CAFE** 103
TIJUANA FLATS 57	**CARROT EXPRESS** 71	**LUNA PARK** 87	**MAX'S GRILLE** 105
COYO TACO 59	**LATIN HOUSE GRILL** 73	**MIAMI GRILL** 89	**MONTY'S RAW BAR** 107
THE RESTAURANT AT W SOUTH BEACH 61	**CARILLON MIAMI** 75	**TAQUIZA** 91	**CAO BAKERY & CAFE** 109
M.E.A.T. EATERY 63	**PURA VIDA** 77	**CUBAN GUYS** 93	**GABE URRUTIA** 115, 119-125
PHUC YEA 65	**33 KITCHEN** 79	**CHEF CHRIS VALDES** 97	**COCONUT CARTEL** 117
	CHEFS ON THE RUN 81	**EATING HOUSE** 99	

TAG THE CREATOR

33 KITCHEN	@33_kitchen	TAQUIZA	@taquizatacos
ARBETTER'S HOT DOGS	@arbetterhotdogs	THE CAFE AT BOOKS & BOOKS	@booksandbooks
BURGER BEAST	@burgerbeast	THE RESTAURANT AT W SOUTH BEACH	@wsouthbeach
CAO BAKERY & CAFE	@caobakery	TIJUANA FLATS	@tijuanaflats
CARILLON MIAMI	@carillonhotel	TRP TASTE	@trptaste
CARROT EXPRESS	@carrotexpress	YOLO	@yolorestaurant
CHEF CHRIS VALDEZ	@chefchrisvaldes		
CHEF JOSE MENDIN	@chefmendin		
CHEF YISUS	@elyisustv		
CHEFS ON THE RUN	@chefsontherun		
CONCERNED COOK	@concernedcook		
COYO TACO	@coyotaco		
CUBAN GUYS	@cubanguys		
DOCE PROVISIONS	@doceprovisions		
DOS CROQUETAS	@doscroquetas		
DRUNKEN DRAGON	@drunkendragon		
EATING HOUSE	@eating_house		
EL REY DE LAS FRITAS	@reydelasfritas		
FINKA TABLE & TAP	@finkatableandtap		
GABRIEL URRUTIA (COCKTAILS)	@looksmelltaste		
GET REAL	@getrealmeals		
HONEYBEE DOUGHNUTS	@honeybeedoughnuts		
HUAHUA'S TAQUERIA	@huahuastaqueria		
LATIN AMERICAN BAKERY & CAFE	@latinamerican_bakery		
LATIN HOUSE GRILL	@latinhousegrill		
LUNA PARK	@lunaparkmiami		
M.E.A.T. EATERY	@meateaterykeys		
MAX'S GRILLE	@maxs_grille		
MIAMI GRILL	@miamigrill		
MONTY'S RAW BAR	@montysrawbarcg		
NAKED TACO	@lovenakedtaco		
PHUC YEA	@phucyea		
PINCHO	@pincho		
PURA VIDA	@puravidamiami		
RAW JUCE	@rawjuce		
SERGIO'S RESTAURANT	@sergiosrestaurant		
SMOKEY BONES	@smokeybonesbar		
KUSH BY STEPHEN'S	@kushhialeah		
SUSHI MAKI	@gosushimaki		
SUVICHE	@suviche		

DON'T FORGET TO CHEF & SHARE

TAG US @TASTEOFMIAMI
AND USE THE #MIAMITASTESSOGOOD
WITH ALL YOUR MASTERPIECES FROM THE BOOK

SMALL B

TES, BRO

BERRY HEMP BANANA ACAI BOWL

SERVING: 1   PREP TIME: 5 MIN

INGREDIENTS

BOWL BASE
8 ounces banana, frozen
4 ounces of mango, frozen
1¾ ounces acai, frozen
4 ounces almond milk

BOWL TOPPINGS
½ cup fresh banana, sliced
¼ cup strawberries, chopped
¼ cup blueberries
1 tablespoon hemp seeds
1 tablespoon almonds, chopped
1 tablespoon cacao nibs
Honey, drizzle to garnish

DIRECTIONS

Blend all base items in your blender for approximately 45 seconds, and scoop contents into a bowl.

Place the slices of banana around the bowl, then add in the hemp seeds and chopped almonds, followed by the strawberries and blueberries. Finish with the cacao nibs and drizzle of honey.

RAW JUCE

CHORIZO CROQUETA

YIELDS: 30 PIECES **PREP TIME: 25 MIN** **COOK TIME: 25 MIN**

SPECIAL TOOLS: Deep fryer, 4-quart rondeau pan or braising pan; food processor or meat grinding attachment for stand mixer.

INGREDIENTS

- 2 ounces of unsalted butter
- 2 shallots, finely chopped
- 8 garlic cloves, finely chopped
- 4 ounces applewood-smoked bacon, ground
- 8 ounces Chorizo Cantimpalo, ground
- 4 ounces smoked pork loin, ground
- 4 ounces heavy cream
- 8 ounces milk
- 1 tablespoon smoked paprika
- 1 tablespoon complete seasoning
- 12 ounces all-purpose flour
- 4 eggs
- 8 ounces Italian breadcrumbs, finely ground
- Vegetable oil for deep-frying (amount will vary depending on pot size)
- Salt and pepper to taste

DIRECTIONS

Melt the butter in a large pot over medium heat. Add the shallot and garlic. Simmer until fragrant.

Add the bacon and cook until rendered, about 4-5 minutes. Add the chorizo and smoked pork loin; continue to cook for about 3 minutes. Add the cream and milk; bring to a boil, then turn the heat to low. Add the paprika and complete seasoning. Add the flour in four additions and cook until incorporated and no lumps remain. Taste for seasoning.

Transfer the mixture to a sheet pan and let cool. While the mixture is still warm, transfer it to a large piping bag and cut the tip ¾-inch wide. Pipe onto a 13x18-inch baking sheet and score with a knife at 2-inch intervals. Freeze until firm, 1 hour.

Cut through the scored sections and then roll the individual croquetas by hand to make them even. Whisk together the eggs in a shallow dish until combined. Place the breadcrumbs in a separate shallow dish and set aside.

Dip the croquetas in the egg mixture, place on a baking sheet to drain the excess egg, and then toss lightly in the breadcrumb mixture.

Place the breaded croquetas on a sheet pan and freeze.

Heat vegetable oil in a deep fryer to 350°F. Fry the croquetas until golden brown, 4-5 minutes.

DOCE PROVISIONS

CONCH FRITTERS

SERVINGS: 4 PREP TIME: 90 MIN COOK TIME: 6 MIN

SPECIAL TOOLS: Stand mixer with grinder attachment; flour sifter

INGREDIENTS

1 pound cleaned conch
4 ounces ripe banana
¼ cup red onion, ¼-inch dice
¼ cup poblano pepper, ¼-inch dice
¼ cup red bell pepper, ¼-inch dice
1 teaspoon curry powder
1 tablespoon unsalted butter
1½ teaspoon kosher salt
1 egg
¼ cup half & half
5 ounces all-purpose flour
1 teaspoon baking powder

MANGO BROWN BUTTER
2 ounces red onion, diced
1 vanilla bean, split and scraped
1 cup dark rum
1 tablespoon aji amarillo paste
½ cup cider vinegar
½ cup granulated sugar
1 ounce ginger root, peeled and sliced
1 cup mango puree
10 ounces unsalted butter
1 tablespoon kosher salt

DIRECTIONS

Remember to keep the conch refrigerated during this process.

Grind conch meat and bananas together.

Sauté onion and peppers with butter, curry, and salt over medium heat until onions are translucent. Spread on paper-lined pan to cool.

Place eggs and half & half into the blender and pulse 6-8 times.

Combine banana/conch mixture, cooled vegetables, and egg mixture in a large mixing bowl. Stir with hands until combined.

Sift flour and baking powder into a bowl and continue to mix with hands until just combined.

Form into smooth 1 ounce balls and fry at 300°F for 5 minutes. Cool on sheet pans in a single layer.

MANGO BROWN BUTTER
In a saucepan over medium heat combine rum, vinegar, sugar, red onion, vanilla, pepper and ginger. Reduce by half, add mango puree, and cook for 10 minutes more.

Remove from heat and cool slightly.

In a separate pan, brown butter and add to mixture.

Remove vanilla bean and ginger, and place in blender.

Place on low and turn on, slowly increase speed to high.

Top off the fritters with a drizzle of Mango Brown Butter Sauce and serve a side for extra dipping.

TRP TASTE

ELOTE

SERVING: 1   PREP TIME: 5 MIN   COOK TIME: 10 MIN

SPECIAL TOOLS: Grill

INGREDIENTS

ELOTE DRESSING
½ cup mayonnaise
1 tablespoon water
1 tablespoon lime juice
Small pinch salt
½ teaspoon chili powder
½ teaspoon smoked paprika
¼ teaspoon chili powder or 1 tablespoon spicy smoky Adobo sauce

ELOTE
1 ear fresh corn
½ ounce elote dressing
2 ounces Cotija cheese
½ ounce Tajín
1 ounce cilantro, chopped
1 lime wedge

DIRECTIONS

Prepare the grill to a high temperature.

Pull husk away from corn cob and remove silks. To create a handle, insert a bamboo stick.

Grill corn, turning every 2-3 minutes (up to 10 minutes) until slightly charred on all sides.

In a small bowl, whisk together mayonnaise, water, paprika, chili powder, salt, and lime juice.

Brush Elote Dressing over grilled corn, covering every kernel.

Sprinkle Cotija cheese around the grilled corn as it will stick to the elote dressing.

Sprinkle with cilantro and Tajín.

Serve accompanied with a lime wedge.

HUAHUA'S TAQUERIA

GRILLED SHRIMP & AVOCADO TARTINE

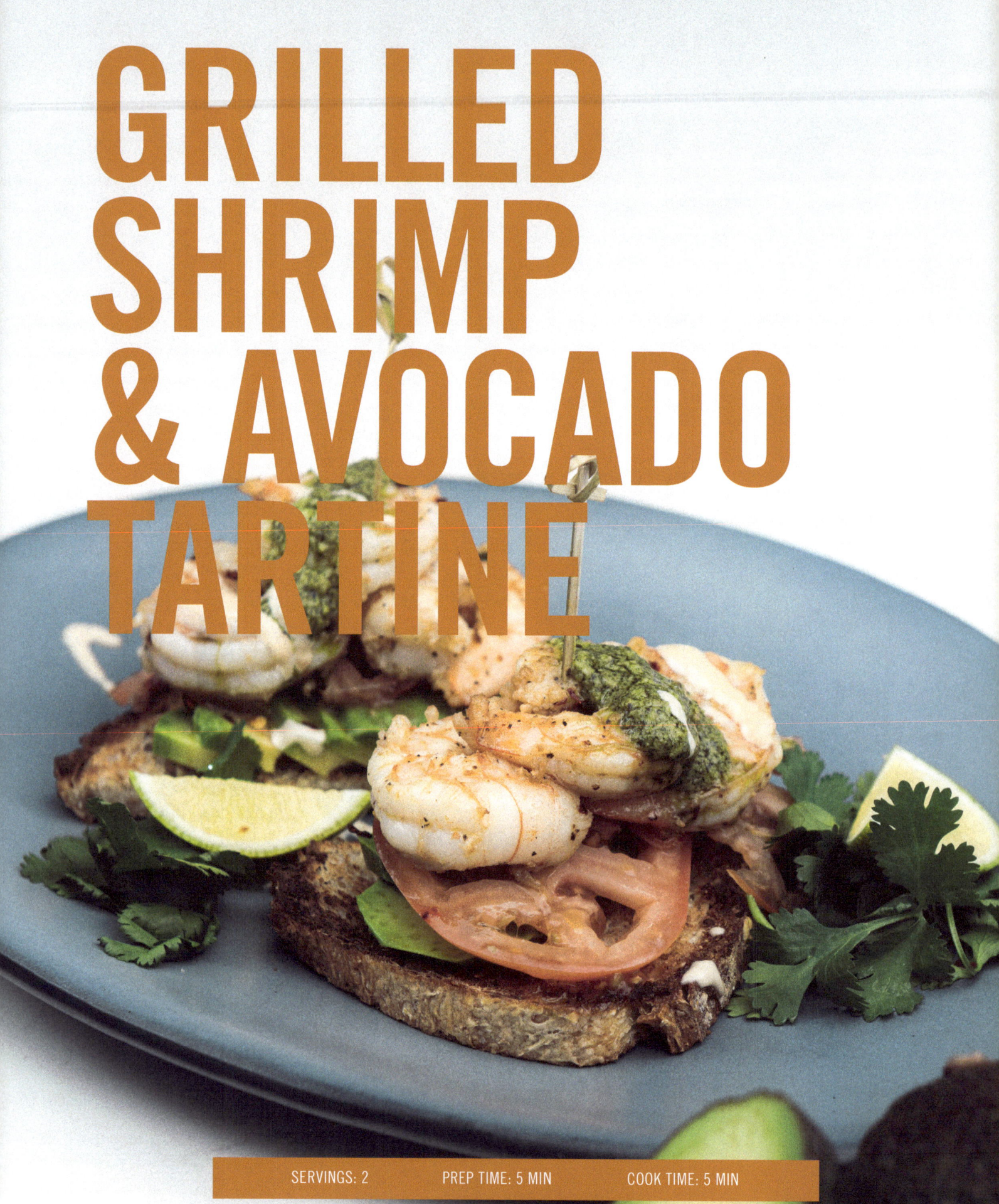

SERVINGS: 2 PREP TIME: 5 MIN COOK TIME: 5 MIN

SPECIAL TOOLS: Griddle Pan

INGREDIENTS

12 large Key West pink shrimp, peeled and deveined
¼ teaspoon ground cumin
¼ teaspoon kosher salt
¼ teaspoon freshly ground black pepper
1 tablespoon extra-virgin olive oil
1 ripe avocado, peeled and sliced
1 teaspoon lemon juice
4 thick slices whole-grain country bread
⅛ teaspoon crushed red pepper flakes
1 small heirloom tomato, sliced
1 tablespoon basil pesto
1 tablespoon garlic aioli
4 sprigs cilantro

DIRECTIONS

GRILLED SHRIMP
Heat a nonstick griddle to medium-high heat.

Season the shrimp with cumin, salt, and pepper.

Heat the olive oil on the griddle until it just begins to shimmer and add shrimp, cooking each side for about 2-3 minutes or until they turn a rosy pink.

PREPARE THE TOAST
Toast the bread golden brown. Slice the avocado and divide it amongst the toast. Drizzle with lemon juice and season with salt and crushed red pepper. Layer each with the tomato slices and arrange shrimp on top.

To serve: Spoon basil pesto over shrimp and drizzle the tartines with garlic aioli. Garnish with cilantro.

THE CAFE AT BOOKS & BOOKS

HEART OF PALM CEVICHE

SERVINGS: 5-6 | PREP TIME: 30 MIN | COOK TIME: 5 MIN

SPECIAL TOOLS: Scale

INGREDIENTS

LECHE DE TIGRE
20 grams celery
20 grams white onion
10 grams ginger, peeled
3 garlic cloves
3 grams cilantro, chopped
50 grams heart of palm
250 milliliters water
200 milliliters lime juice
100 grams of ice cubes
25 grams kosher salt

CEVICHE
32 ounces of heart of palm, diced in medium-size rounds
4 teaspoons kosher salt
4 tablespoons cilantro, finely chopped (leaves only)
Leche de Tigre
2 limes
3 ounces red onion, julienne

DIRECTIONS

LECHE DE TIGRE
Combine all ingredients in a blender.

Pulse until all ingredients are well combined.

Strain mixture and skim foam from the top of the liquid by using a spoon.

Refrigerate until used for ceviche.

CEVICHE
In a bowl combine the heart of palm, salt, cilantro, and lime juice. Mix well, being careful not to break the hearts of palm.

Add vegan Leche de Tigre sauce and red onions to the bowl, mix well.

NOTE: Feel free to add some crispy plantain chips or tortilla chips as the crunch will go well with the ceviche.

SUVICHE

MIXED SEAFOOD CEVICHE

SERVINGS: 1-2   PREP TIME: 10 MIN

INGREDIENTS

PROTEINS
1 ounce shrimp 16/20, peeled & deveined
1 ounce bay scallops 20/30
3 ounces white fish

COMPONENTS
1 ounce baby heirloom tomatoes
2 ounces red onion, julienne
4 grams cancha
½ key lime
3-5 jalapeño slices
4 grams of micro cilantro
1 bamboo leaf

SAUCE
3 ounces agua chile
32 ounces amazu
3 guajillo chile
1 arbol chile
64 ounces watermelon
2 ounces yuzu
Salt to taste

SEAFOOD BLANCH STOCK
1 carrot
2 yellow onions
1 celery
1 bunch bay leaf
Salt to taste
2 lemons
Old Bay to taste
Black pepper to taste

DIRECTIONS

To make Sauce: blend all at medium/high until color changes and it's smooth.

To make Seafood Blanch Stock: Blanch proteins separately, then toss in an ice bath.

To prep Ceviche: Add all components to the mixing bowl and mix in the sauce. Place a bamboo leaf on the plate and plate ceviche mix on top of the leaf. Garnish with micro cilantro on top and key lime on the side.

CHEF JOSE MENDIN

PARMESAN BRUSSELS SPROUTS W. CHIMICHURRI

SERVINGS: 4   PREP TIME: 10 MIN   COOK TIME: 30 MIN

INGREDIENTS

CHIMICHURRI
¼ cup fresh parsley, chopped
2 tablespoons minced garlic
3 tablespoons red pepper flakes
2 tablespoons dried oregano
½ cup olive oil (or sunflower/vegetable oil)
¼ cup red wine vinegar
Pinch of salt

PARMESAN BRUSSELS SPROUTS
1 pound brussels sprouts
¼ cup parmesan cheese
¼ cup chimichurri
2 tablespoons olive oil
Pinch of salt

DIRECTIONS

CHIMICHURRI
In a small bowl, mix parsley, garlic, red pepper flakes, oregano, and salt together.

Add oil and vinegar to the bowl and mix thoroughly. Refrigerate overnight for best flavor.

PARMESAN BRUSSELS SPROUTS
Preheat the oven to 400°F.

Rinse brussels sprouts, tear out any leaves that seem yellow or blemished, cut off the bottom stem, and slice them in half.

In a large bowl, add brussels sprouts, olive oil, salt, and parmesan cheese; mix evenly until all brussels sprouts are coated with oil and parmesan cheese.

Put brussels sprouts on a baking sheet spaced out to make sure they're not crowding one another. Roast in the oven for 30-40 minutes until crispy and lightly charred on the outside.

Halfway through cooking, use a spatula to toss the brussels sprouts so they cook evenly.

Once ready, serve on a large dish and drizzle chimichurri over the crispy sprouts.

CONCERNED COOK

REUBEN CROQUETA

YIELDS: 42 PIECES   PREP TIME: 45 MIN   COOK TIME: 6-8 MIN

INGREDIENTS

6 tablespoons butter
2 cups sauerkraut, strained
1 cup onion, chopped
6 tablespoons minced garlic
3 pounds corned beef
2 pounds Swiss cheese
3 pounds rye breadcrumbs
8 eggs, lightly beaten

DIRECTIONS

In a food processor or blender, pulverize rye bread until fine. Place in a bowl and set aside.

In a food processor or blender, mix butter, onions, garlic powder, sauerkraut, corned beef, and cheese.

Beat 4 eggs and 3 cups of breading into the mixture.

Mix all ingredients by hand until they are evenly dispersed.

Weigh out 1½ ounce portions and shape the croquetas into a cylindrical form. Place on an oiled sheet pan and cool for 15-20 minutes.

Beat remaining eggs and place them in a bowl.

Place the remaining 3 cups of breadcrumbs in a bowl.

Dip chilled croquetas into the egg wash, then breadcrumbs and place in the freezer.

Once croquetas are frozen, fry at 350°F until golden brown.

KUSH BY STEPHEN'S

SPECIAL TOOLS: Food Processor

INGREDIENTS

1 package of dumpling wrappers (50 pieces)
14 ounces of peeled and deveined shrimp, finely chopped
2 ounces chicken fat (preferably chicken skin)
2 tablespoons dark soy sauce
1 medium garlic clove, minced
2½ teaspoons peeled fresh ginger, minced
½ teaspoon ground white pepper
1 teaspoon Asian sesame oil
1 teaspoon Shaoxing cooking wine
1 cup of water

DIRECTIONS

In a food processor or mixing bowl, add chopped shrimp, chicken fat, minced garlic, and ginger, white pepper, soy sauce, sesame oil, and cooking wine.

Take a dumpling wrapper and place a tablespoon of the mixture in the middle.

Dip your finger in a bit of water and moisten the outer edges of half the dumpling wrapper in a semicircle. Fold dumpling wrapper in half, evenly.

Use the palm of your hand to flatten the bottom of the dumpling, so it sits upright. Pinch wrapper and seal so that all seams are sealed.

Add oil to a nonstick frying pan on high heat and sear dumplings bottom down until browned, approximately 3 minutes.

Add a ¼ cup of water to the pan and immediately cover with a lid. Steam dumplings for 2 minutes (or until most of the water evaporates).

Repeat the process to your liking.

NOTE: We recommend searing 5-9 dumplings at a time, depending on the size of the pan used.

DRUNKEN DRAGON

SNAPPER CEVICHE

SERVINGS: 4   **PREP TIME: 60 MIN**

INGREDIENTS

1 pound of snapper filets:
    pin bones and blood line removed
    cut into ¾-inch cubes
2 tablespoons red onion, brunoises
2 tablespoons daikon radish, brunoises
2 tablespoons celery, brunoises
1 tablespoon Fresno pepper, brunoises
2 tablespoons red bell pepper, brunoises
2 tablespoons corn, shucked

1 cup fresh-squeezed lime juice
½ teaspoon garlic, minced
½ teaspoon ginger, minced
½ tablespoon celery, minced
½ ounce of snapper
2½ teaspoons mango puree
1 teaspoon aji amarillo puree
1 tablespoon kosher salt

DIRECTIONS

Remember to keep the fish refrigerated during this process.

Gently fold the following in a bowl:
    1 pound snapper filet
    2 tablespoons red onion
    2 tablespoons daikon radish
    2 tablespoons celery
    1 tablespoon Fresno pepper
    2 tablespoons red bell pepper
    2 tablespoons corn

Place the following in a blender:
    1 cup lime juice
    ½ teaspoon garlic
    ½ teaspoon ginger
    ½ tablespoon celery
    ½ ounce fish (same as used for the ceviche)
    2½ teaspoons mango puree
    1 teaspoon aji amarillo puree
    1 tablespoon kosher salt

Puree until smooth (approximately 15-20 seconds).

Pour the contents of the blender over the contents of the bowl, gently fold to combine, and chill for at least one hour before serving.

YOLO

SPICY TUNA SALAD

SERVINGS: 1   PREP TIME: 10 MIN

INGREDIENTS

4 ounces fresh, sushi-grade tuna cut in ½-inch cubes
½ of a Hass avocado, cubed into ½-inch pieces
1 teaspoon kimchee sauce
½ teaspoon sesame oil
2 cups of field greens (romaine and spring mix)
2 ounces balsamic vinaigrette
¼ cucumber, thinly sliced
4 cherry tomatoes, halved
¼ teaspoon of sesame seeds
2 ounces of shredded carrots

DIRECTIONS

Cut tuna and avocado into ½-inch cubes and place into a small mixing bowl.

Add kimchee sauce, sushi vinegar, and sesame oil to tuna and avocado. Gently mix ingredients.

In a separate mixing bowl, toss romaine lettuce with balsamic vinaigrette.

Place greens onto a generously sized serving plate.

Top the greens with the tuna and avocado mix and garnish with cucumbers, tomato, and shredded carrots.

Sprinkle sesame seeds for finishing touch.

SUSHI MAKI

SUNDAY BRUNCH CROQUETA

YIELDS: 20-25 PIECES   PREP/COOK TIME: 1 HR   TOTAL TIME: 3 HRS

INGREDIENTS

4 TBSP unsalted butter
1 TBSP olive oil
2/3 cup all-purpose flour
2 cups whole milk, room temperature

MIX-INS
½ cup leeks, finely chopped (tender green & white part)
8 ounces ground chorizo
4 hard-boiled eggs, diced
1 heaping TBSP Italian flat-leaf parsley, finely chopped

SPICES
1½ TSP Spanish smoked paprika
¼ TSP onion powder
1 TSP kosher salt
¼ TSP black pepper
Additional salt and pepper to taste

BREADING STATION (using separate bowls for each)
DRY: 1 cup all-purpose flour
    Seasoned with salt & pepper
WET: 2 eggs, well-beaten
DRY: 2 cups of Panko crumbs, pulsed in a food processor
    ¼ cup of grated parmesan cheese
    Seasoned with salt & pepper

DIRECTIONS

Gather, measure, and organize all your ingredients and utensils. Have on-hand a whisk, wooden spoon or high heat spatula, medium sauté pan, and shallow dish for croqueta mixture (masa) to chill.

On medium heat, add 8 ounces of ground chorizo to the pan and sauté 3-4 minutes until cooked. With a slotted spoon, remove and reserve the cooked chorizo. Do not clean out the pan.

In the same pan, on low-medium heat, add 4 tablespoons of butter, 1 tablespoon of olive oil, leeks, and a pinch of salt and pepper. Sauté until leeks are translucent 1-2 minutes.

Add 2/3 cup of flour to the sautéed leeks and use a wooden spoon to mix well and lightly toast the flour, constantly stirring and breaking up any lumps that may occur in the flour.

Make sure that flour is toasting and not browning for 2 minutes, cooking out the raw flour taste.

Slowly pour the milk, constantly stirring/whisking to fully incorporate the milk, again breaking up any lumps of flour to create the béchamel.

Add the ¼ teaspoon of onion powder, 1½ teaspoon of Spanish smoked paprika, 1 teaspoon of salt, and ¼ teaspoon of black pepper. Continue stirring to develop flavor and scraping the bottom of the pan with a wooden spoon to ensure that the béchamel is not sticking to the pan.

Stir the béchamel for approximately 5-10 minutes. The mixture will begin to thicken into a paste (this is normal), continue stirring, and working the mixture until it pulls away from the sides of the pan. Check heat and adjust if need be. It is a slow and steady cooking method while working the mixture to create a smooth and creamy texture.

Add the cooked chorizo, working it into the mixture, or masa, until fully incorporated. The chorizo will release more of its flavor into the whole masa, again building the layers of flavor.

Add 1 heaping tablespoon of finely chopped flat-leaf parsley and incorporate it into the mixture.
Turn off heat and add the diced egg and gently mix in, careful not to fully mash the egg. You want to retain as much of the small pieces of egg whites.

Taste and adjust seasoning with salt and pepper.

Remove the masa and place it in a shallow dish, press directly onto the mixture with plastic wrap, and chill for a few hours or until very firm.

Remove the chilled mixture from the refrigerator and scoop out approximately 1-ounce portions with a small spoon or small scooper for evenly sized croquetas. Roll into the desired shape, balls, or 2-inch cylinders.

One by one, coat each croqueta with seasoned flour, dredge in egg-wash and then coat in the panko/parmesan breading, pressing lightly to cover the entire croqueta.

Fry in peanut oil or canola oil at 350°F for 2 minutes or until golden brown.
Let cool for 2 minutes before serving.

DOS CROQUETAS

HAY HA

AMBRE

ABUELA'S HAM AND CHORIZO CUBAN MACARONI

SERVINGS: 10 PREP TIME: 15 MIN COOK TIME: 30-35 MIN

SPECIAL TOOLS: Large baking dish

INGREDIENTS

16 ounces tomato sauce
16 ounces marinara sauce
3 pounds of cavatappi pasta
2 pounds boneless ham steak, cubed
½ pound Spanish chorizo, cubed
8 ounces yellow onion, finely chopped
4 ounces green peppers, finely chopped
1 ounce garlic, finely chopped
1 tablespoon olive oil
4 ounces white wine
2 ounces salt
1 ounce sugar
Pinch of oregano
3 ounces parmesan cheese
3 ounces mozzarella cheese
Pinch of parsley

DIRECTIONS

Preheat the oven to 350°F.

Heat a large sauté pan to medium-high heat, and add a tablespoon of olive oil. Begin cooking the sofrito; a combination of garlic, onion, and peppers. Cook until onions are translucent and soft—about 5 minutes.

Add ham and chorizo, cooking for 2-3 minutes.

Add tomato sauce, sugar, salt, oregano, and white wine to the pan. Cook at low heat for 15-20 minutes.

Bring a large pot of salted water and a few drops of olive oil to a boil. Cook pasta to your preference. Drain and add to the sauté pan. Mix together.

Place pasta in a large baking dish and top with mozzarella and parmesan cheese. Bake in the oven for 10 minutes or until the cheese has melted and browned.

Garnish with a pinch of chopped parsley.

SERGIO'S RESTAURANT

BEAST-LOAF

SERVINGS: 8   PREP TIME: 10-15 MIN   COOK TIME: 50 MIN

INGREDIENTS

2 pounds sirloin ground beef (90/10)
1 cup seasoned breadcrumbs
2 eggs
¼ teaspoon ground pepper
⅛ teaspoon smoked paprika
⅛ teaspoon cayenne pepper
8 ounces white onion, finely diced
1 cup Guava Sriracha Ketchup BEAST Sauce

NOTE: BEAST Sauce available for purchase on burgerbeastsauce.com

DIRECTIONS

Preheat the oven to 350°F.

In a large bowl add beef, breadcrumbs, eggs, pepper, paprika, cayenne pepper, diced onions, and ½ cup of BEAST sauce. Mix with hands until combined well, but don't overdo it.

Move the mixture to a cutting board and shape to your liking.

Carefully slide the BEAST-loaf onto a baking sheet.

Take another ½ cup of BEAST Sauce and spoon it over the beauty.

Place your creation in the preheated oven and bake for approximately 55 minutes. The internal temperature should reach 160°F when done.

Let it rest for 10 minutes before digging in.

BURGER BEAST

BIG BEEF RIBS

SERVINGS: 4   **PREP TIME: 30 MIN**   **COOK TIME: 8-9 HRS**

SPECIAL TOOLS: Smoker or charcoal grill setup for indirect cooking

INGREDIENTS

BIG BEEF RIB
6 pounds Short Rib Plate (3-bone beef ribs) **see NOTE**
½ cup kosher salt and ground black pepper (50/50 mixture)
12 ounces water in a clean spray bottle

GARLIC-HERB SAUCE
6 ounces olive oil
3 tablespoons parsley, finely chopped
2 tablespoons garlic, minced
4 teaspoons red wine vinegar
½ teaspoon kosher salt
¼ teaspoon black pepper, ground

DIRECTIONS

BIG BEEF RIB
Remove the short rib plate from packaging and pat dry with clean paper towels.

Place on a sheet pan and lightly cover it with plastic wrap. Allow to sit out at room temperature for 2 hours.

When the 2 hours have passed, season the short rib plate with the salt and pepper mixture. Lightly press in the seasoning and ensure that all edges and tips are evenly seasoned.

Prepare your smoker or charcoal grill with a combination of lump charcoal and hardwood such as hickory, pecan, or oak. The temperature should be between 225°F-250°F.

Place short rib plate in the smoker or grill to cook, adding wood as needed over the course of the approximately 8-hour cook time.

At the 5-hour mark, begin spraying the plate with water on the edges/high spots to keep from drying out and overcooking. Spray once an hour for the remainder of the cooking time.

Cook to an internal temperature of 200°F measured in the thickest part of the plate and/or between the bones. When touching the plate, the cap and meat should feel soft and "jiggly" almost like softened butter.

When the plate is finished cooking, transfer to a pan, and partially cover the pan with foil. Allow it to rest for at least 30 minutes before slicing.

Serve with the garlic-herb sauce or another of your favorites along with your choice of sides.

GARLIC-HERB SAUCE
Place all ingredients in a small mixing bowl and stir until completely incorporated.

Serve along with the beef rib. The bright and acidic qualities of the sauce do well with the rich, indulgent beef rib.

NOTE: You will need to order this cut from your specialty grocer or butcher. This is a Beef Plate Short Rib not a Beef Chuck Short Rib (this cut has 3 bones as opposed to 4 bones on a typical Chuck Short Rib).

SMOKEY BONES

BLACKENED FISH TACOS

YIELDS: 6 TACOS　　PREP TIME: 25-35 MIN　　COOK TIME: 5-10 MIN

SPECIAL TOOLS: Blender or Food Processor

INGREDIENTS

BLACKENED FISH
1 pound of mahi-mahi
3 tablespoons blackening spice:
    1 tablespoon light brown sugar
    1 tablespoon ground cayenne
    1 tablespoon dried oregano
    1 tablespoon sweet paprika
    1 tablespoon dried cilantro
    1 tablespoon black pepper
    1 tablespoon sea salt

TROPICAL FRUIT SALSA
2 juicy sweet mangos, diced
1 cup fresh pineapple, diced
1 sweet red pepper, diced
1 sweet yellow pepper, diced
1 jalapeño pepper, diced
2 green onions, thinly sliced
2-3 tablespoons fresh cilantro, chopped
4 ounces fresh lime juice
4 ounces virgin olive oil

AVOCADO CREMA
4 ounces sour cream
4 ounces mayonnaise
1 ripe avocado, mashed
2 ounces fresh lime juice
Salt and pepper

TORTILLAS
6 flour or corn tortillas

DIRECTIONS

Cut the fish into 6 equal portions according to the size of your tortilla.

Rub the fish with olive oil and then season the fish with the blackening spice by rubbing it into the fish delicately.

Before cooking the fish, assemble the tropical fruit salsa by combining all the ingredients, and then season with salt and black pepper.

In a food processor or blender, mix the ingredients for the avocado crema until creamy.

Prepare the fish in a nonstick pan, a grill, or a toaster oven. Cook the fish for about 3-5 minutes until done—keeping it juicy and moist.

Remove the fish from the heat and sprinkle it with lime juice, fresh cilantro, and salt.

ASSEMBLE THE TACOS
Warm the tortillas on both sides with a nonstick pan or a grill.

For the base, add lime crema in the tortilla first.

Add the fish.

Top the fish with the tropical fruit salsa.

NAKED TACO

CHICKEN CACCIATORE

SERVINGS: 4-6 **PREP TIME: 20 MIN** **COOK TIME: 5-10 MIN**

INGREDIENTS

2-3 pounds chicken thighs
¼ cup olive oil
½ large onion, chopped
2-3 cloves of garlic, chopped

BREADING
½ cup flour
1 teaspoon salt
½ teaspoon black pepper

TOMATO SAUCE
28 ounces whole tomatoes, canned
1 teaspoon salt
1 teaspoon oregano
½ teaspoon black pepper
½ teaspoon crushed red pepper
1 teaspoon parsley, chopped

PEPPERS AND MUSHROOMS
2-3 tablespoons butter
½ red pepper, chopped
½ green pepper, chopped
½ pound mushrooms, sliced
1-2 tablespoons red wine

DIRECTIONS

In a large bowl, mix all breading ingredients and lightly coat chicken.

In a blender, blend whole tomatoes, salt, pepper, oregano, red pepper, and parsley.

Using a large skillet, add oil and bring to medium-high heat.

Add chicken skin side down. Brown all sides and turn as necessary.

When all sides of chicken are browned, add onions and garlic. Continue to cook until garlic is lightly toasted and onions are tender. Reduce to medium heat.

Slowly add tomato mixture from the blender to the skillet. Continue to cook 20-30 minutes until chicken is tender and cooked all the way through.

While the chicken is cooking, in a small skillet add butter, peppers, and mushrooms. Cook over medium heat until mushrooms are brown and peppers start to soften.

When peppers and mushrooms are finished browning, add to the chicken and tomato sauce.

Lastly, add red or burgundy wine. Cook down wine (around 5 minutes) and enjoy.

NOTE: Best served over angel hair pasta.

ARBETTER'S HOT DOGS

CHIMICHURRI STEAK TACOS

YIELDS: 12 TACOS   PREP TIME: 45-60 MIN   COOK TIME: 15-20 MIN

INGREDIENTS

MOJO MARINATED STEAK
4 cloves of garlic, peeled
½ cup fresh-squeezed lime juice
½ cup cilantro, chopped
2 teaspoons kosher salt
1 teaspoon cumin
1 cup canola oil
2 pounds choice steaks, ½-inch thick
1½ teaspoons of kosher salt
½ teaspoon of cracked black pepper

12 white corn tortillas
Shredded lettuce

CHIMICHURRI SAUCE
6 cloves garlic, peeled, whole
1 jalapeño pepper, discard seeds
1 bunch of cilantro
1 bunch of parsley
2 tablespoons fresh lime juice
½ cup canola oil
½ teaspoon dark chili powder
1 teaspoon kosher salt

CHARRED CORN SALSA
4 ears of fresh corn, shucked and silk removed
2 tablespoons canola oil
2 teaspoons fine sea salt
1 teaspoon dark chile powder
½ cup diced tomatoes
¼ cup diced yellow onions
2 tablespoons diced poblano pepper
2 tablespoons of fresh lime juice
1 tablespoon chopped cilantro
½ teaspoon kosher salt

DIRECTIONS

MOJO MARINADE
Combine all ingredients (except oil) into a food processor, and pulse 3-4 times to combine.

Turn processor on and drizzle oil into mixture until fully blended.

Remove from the processor, place in a container, and store in the refrigerator until needed.

STEAKS
Marinate steaks in the refrigerator for 3 hours (or up to 24 hours) before cooking. Place steak in a gallon zippered bag and combine with 1 cup of mojo marinade.

Season marinated steaks on each side with salt and pepper. Let sit for 30 minutes to come to room temperature before grilling.

Set the grill to medium-high and when it's hot, lay the steaks on the hottest part of the grill and sear, flipping every 2 minutes until the desired doneness is reached.

Remove steaks from the grill and let rest on a plate for 10-15 minutes.

Dice all steaks into ½ inch thick pieces, then place back on to plate without the wire rack.

CHIMICHURRI SAUCE
Set the oven rack to the highest level and preheat to broil on high.

Rinse, core, and seed peppers. Place jalapeño peppers and garlic cloves on a foil-lined baking pan and broil until well charred, about 5 minutes, rotating halfway through. Remove from the oven and let cool.

Rough chop cilantro and parsley, removing about 2 inches of stems, and set aside.

Once cooled, rough chop jalapeño and garlic, then place into a food processor and pulse 3-4 times until roughly pureed. Add remaining ingredients and process until smooth.

Empty sauce into bowl and taste for seasoning level. Adjust seasoning to your liking.

CORN SALSA
While preheating outdoor grill, brush corn with oil and season with salt and chile powder.

Place on grill and char, rotating corn as necessary throughout. Once charred, remove, and let cool.

Once cooled, use a chef's knife and cutting board to remove corn from cobs and set aside.

Combine the charred corn, tomatoes, onion, pepper, and cilantro in a bowl and season with kosher salt and fresh lime juice to taste.

TO ASSEMBLE
Heat the corn tortillas on the grill for 3-5 seconds per side.

Place a warm tortilla on your plate and top with lettuce.

Add the steak, shredded cheese, corn salsa, and chimichurri sauce.

TIJUANA FLATS

ENCHILADAS DE MARISCOS

SERVINGS: 4-6　　PREP TIME: 1 HR　　COOK TIME: 40 MIN

INGREDIENTS

12 corn tortillas, 6-inch diameter
2 tablespoons butter
1 tablespoon garlic, chopped
2 tablespoons jalapeño pepper, chopped
1 pound cooked shrimp, roughly chopped
1 pound blue crab lump meat, roughly chopped
1 pound cooked lobster meat, roughly chopped
½ cup cilantro, chopped (save ¼ cup for garnish)
1 teaspoon salt or to taste
Mexican crema
2 cups queso fresco, crumbled

GUAJILLO CHILE
2 tablespoons light olive or vegetable oil
6 guajillo chiles (seeds and stems removed), roughly chopped
1 cup white onions, roughly chopped
6 garlic cloves
2 cups canned tomatoes
¼ cup honey
¼ cup cider vinegar
1 cup heavy cream
1 teaspoon salt

DIRECTIONS

SEAFOOD FILLING
In a large skillet on medium-high heat add butter, garlic, onions, and jalapeño. Simmer slowly until onions are translucent. Let cool.

Once cooled, fold in the seafood and half of the chopped cilantro. Season to taste and reserve mixture.

GUAJILLO CHILE
In a medium-sized, heavy-bottom saucepan over medium-high heat, add olive oil and guajillo chiles. Toast the chiles quickly and remove them from the pot (burnt chiles will make your sauce bitter).

Reduce to medium heat, add onions and garlic. Simmer until onions are translucent.

Add chiles back to the saucepan along with tomatoes, honey, and vinegar. Simmer slowly for about 10 minutes.

Add the cream and season with salt, simmering for 10 minutes more. Remove from heat and allow to cool briefly.

Pour sauce mixture into the blender and puree until smooth and creamy. If the sauce appears to be too thick, add more heavy cream as needed. Reserve.

ENCHILADAS
Place a medium-sized skillet over medium-high heat. One at a time, heat the tortillas on both sides. Hold tortillas in aluminum foil to keep warm.

Preheat the oven to 350°F.

Prepare a large baking dish by lightly brushing it with olive oil.

Next, fill each tortilla with a half cup of the seafood mixture. Roll the tortilla tightly and place it with the seam side down into the baking dish. Continue rolling all 12.

Spoon sauce over enchiladas to coat each one and cover with aluminum foil. Bake for 30 minutes until warmed through.

Remove aluminum foil and sprinkle the tops of the enchiladas with queso fresco, and return the pan into the oven for 10 minutes uncovered until the cheese is warm.

With a spatula, carefully remove the enchiladas from the pan to a plate-- two enchiladas per plate. Spoon crema over each set of enchiladas and garnish with chopped cilantro.

Place the remaining warm sauce on the side, so guests can add more as needed.

COYO TACO

GNOCCHI AL PESTO

SERVINGS: 2-4 **PREP TIME: 30 MIN** **COOK TIME: 25 MIN**

SPECIAL TOOLS: Food mill

INGREDIENTS

BASIL PESTO
2 cups Italian basil leaves
1 cup pecorino cheese, grated
3 tablespoons parmigiano cheese, grated
3 tablespoons pine nuts, toasted
1¼ cup extra virgin olive oil
1 clove garlic
Salt to taste

POTATO GNOCCHI
3 pounds russet potato
12 ounces all-purpose flour
2 large eggs
4 ounces parmigiano cheese, grated
1 tablespoon kosher salt
1 teaspoon white pepper, ground
1 teaspoon nutmeg, ground
4 ounces unsalted butter
4 sage leaves

DIRECTIONS

BASIL PESTO
Blanch the basil leaves in hot water for 30 seconds. Cool them down immediately in an ice bath (ice and water). When cold, remove from the ice bath and strain, squeezing to remove excess water.

Add blanched basil, garlic, and pine nuts to a blender with half of the extra virgin oil, and add 2-3 ice cubes to keep the temperature down (and maintain a brilliant green color). Pulse and keep adding oil until smooth. Add cheese and mix until incorporated. Set aside.

POTATO GNOCCHI
Boil whole potatoes (skin on) in abundantly salted water. Remove when cooked (poke the potato with a fork to test the tenderness) and set aside in the refrigerator to cool down. Once cold, peel them and pass them through a food mill. In the meantime, bring butter to simmer with sage leaves for 3 minutes until the butter starts to change color to brown. Set aside.

Prepare a well with the potato over a clean table surface, add all other ingredients in the middle of the well and mix all ingredients. Knead until the dough doesn't stick to the surface.
NOTE: In potatoes, the levels of moisture changes based on how ripe they are. You may need to add more flour. With your hands, roll pieces of dough into a 1-inch thick roll, and then cut diagonally into 1-inch long dumplings.

On a lightly floured surface, roll out the dough using your fingertips. The rope of dough should be approximately ¾-inch thick. Cut the rope into ¾-inch pieces.

Use your hands to shape the gnocchi into a slight "C" shape and slightly dust with flour.

Boil dumplings in salted boiling water for 2 minutes (until they float to the surface).

Strain, toss with butter sage sauce, sprinkle with grated parmigiano, and serve.

THE RESTAURANT AT W SOUTH BEACH

GUAVA BBQ RIBS

SERVINGS: 4-6 — PREP TIME: 9 HRS — COOK TIME: 4.5-6.5 HRS

SPECIAL TOOLS: Smoker

INGREDIENTS

GUAVA BBQ SAUCE
20 tablespoons garlic, chopped
2½ cups yellow onion, minced
20 tablespoons butter
1 20-ounce container guava paste
20 tablespoons prepared mustard
20 tablespoons brown sugar
10 tablespoons paprika
6 tablespoons allspice
10 tablespoons chili powder
6 tablespoons dried oregano
20 teaspoons dried thyme
10 teaspoons salt
10 cups Mango Chipotle Ketchup

5 cups water
10 cups cider vinegar
20 tablespoons Worcestershire sauce

RIBS
2 racks of pork back ribs
2 tablespoons Rib Rub per rack of rib

NOTE: Mango Chipotle Ketchup is available on meateatery.com

DIRECTIONS

GUAVA BBQ SAUCE
Sauté onions and garlic in butter until softened. Add the rest of the ingredients and bring to a boil. Let cool and transfer to a blender. Puree until smooth and chill.

RIBS
First, we rub the ribs with our Rib Rub which consists of cayenne pepper, brown sugar, paprika, cumin, salt, and black pepper. Let the rub set in for at least 15-20 minutes and then put ribs into the smoker at 280°F for 4 hours. We use a mix of Hickory and Pecan wood chips in our smoker.

Coat generously with Guava BBQ sauce and serve.

M.E.A.T. EATERY

SERVINGS: 2   PREP TIME: 15 MIN   COOK TIME: 10 MIN

INGREDIENTS

1 pound fresh mussels (PEI or Maine), debearded
1 teaspoon green curry paste
¼ cup lemongrass stalk (white part), chopped
1 tablespoon shallots, minced
1 tablespoon fresh garlic, thinly sliced
¼ cup green grapes, sliced
1 cup coconut milk
½ cup white wine
1 cup mixed fresh herbs (cilantro and Vietnamese basil)
Salt and pepper to taste
Olive oil for cooking

DIRECTIONS

Rinse the mussels under cold running water while scrubbing with a vegetable brush. Discard any with broken shells. Debeard.

Heat olive oil in a 6 to 8-quart stockpot. Once smoking, sauté green curry paste for about 2 minutes. Add shallot and garlic to create a base flavor.

Add the mussels and give them a good toss.

Add wine and allow the liquid to reduce by half, then add the coconut milk and rest of the ingredients.

Cover the pot and steam over medium-high for 5 minutes until the mussels open.

Toss mussels around and serve.

Garnish with fresh herbs and grapes. Serve with your favorite garlic toast to soak up all of the sauce.

PHUC YEA

HOMEMADE CUBAN FRITA BURGER

SERVINGS: 6-8 **PREP TIME:** 45 MIN **COOK TIME:** 5 MIN

SPECIAL TOOL: GRIDDLE PAN

INGREDIENTS

FRITA
1 pound ground beef (80/20)
4 ounces ground chorizo
¾ ounces cumin
¾ ounces garlic powder
¾ ounces onion powder
Salt to taste
1 cup tomato sauce

BREAD AND TOPPINGS
1-2 cans of potato sticks
Cuban bread rolls
½ white onion, diced

DIRECTIONS

Measure out ingredients and add them all into a mixing bowl.
Mix thoroughly. Scoop balls and shape into thin patties. Refrigerate for 30 minutes.

Heat griddle on medium-high heat and drizzle with a bit of cooking oil.
Place patty on the griddle and cook for 2½ minutes on each side.

Place patty on a Cuban roll. Top with onions and potato sticks.

EL REY DE LAS FRITAS

JUPIÑA EXPRESS

SERVINGS: 4   PREP TIME: 2 HRS   COOK TIME: 8-10 MIN

INGREDIENTS

JUPIÑA GLAZE
2-liter bottle of Jupiña
½ cup white sugar

CARAMELIZED ONIONS
3 cups red onions
3 tablespoons brown sugar
3 ounces Jupiña Glaze
2 teaspoons red pepper flakes
2 ounces olive oil
1 pinch kosher salt

BURGER PATTY
4 5-ounce burger patties (80/20 for the grill, 75/25 for skillet)
4 brioche buns
4 slices of gruyère cheese
8 ounces Jupiña Glaze Caramelized Onions
8 tablespoons of potato sticks
4 teaspoons burger seasoning
1 ounce cilantro sauce

DIRECTIONS

JUPIÑA GLAZE
Place all ingredients in an 8-quart pot. Set temperature to 300°F or medium heat and cook for 2 hours.

Remove the pot from heat and let it cool for 30 minutes.
Transfer to a glass or hard plastic container until ready to use.

NOTE: Goes great with pancakes, french toast, or waffles.

CARAMELIZED ONIONS
Peel and cut onions in half. Then cut into ½-inch slices (half moons).

Oil a 10-inch sauté pan and place on the burner at medium-high heat.
Add the onions, and spread out evenly to brown them. Stir occasionally, until onions are soft and translucent.

Add the brown sugar and mix together. Once the brown sugar has dissolved, add the Jupiña glaze, and continue to stir for 1 minute.

Remove from heat, add kosher salt, and stir. Set aside until ready to serve.

COOKING
Season burger patty with ½ teaspoon of burger seasoning on each side.

Apply butter on buns and toast in the pan for 3 minutes on the inside and 1 minute on the top side.
Transfer to a plate when ready.

Cook patty on a skillet at 350°F or medium-high for 4 minutes on each side, flipping once for medium-well temperature. Adjust cooking time if a different temp is desired.

Once the patty is flipped, top with gruyère cheese and allow to melt (remaining 4 minutes).
Remove from the pan and get ready to plate.

BUILDING
Place patty with cheese on the bottom bun.

Top with Jupiña glaze caramelized onions, potato sticks, and drizzle with cilantro sauce.
If you like a little more sweetness on your burger, drizzle some extra Jupiña glaze on top.

Set top bun and enjoy.

PINCHO

LEGAL WRAP

SERVINGS: 1   PREP TIME: 20 MIN   COOK TIME: 10 MIN

SPECIAL TOOLS: Grill

INGREDIENTS

Whole wheat wrap
2 ounces jack cheese
1 droplet chipotle sauce

GRILLED CHICKEN
6 ounces chicken breast
1 tablespoon olive oil
1 garlic clove, minced
¼ lime, juiced
Pinch of rosemary
Pinch of oregano
Pinch of thyme

BROWN RICE & BLACK BEANS
1 cup brown rice, cooked
6 ounces black beans, canned
1 ounce tomato, chopped
2 tablespoons vinegar
Pinch of black pepper
Pinch of cayenne
½ teaspoon garlic, minced
½ teaspoon salt

PICO DE GALLO (makes 1½ cups)
3 tomatoes, diced
¼ onion, minced
1½ tablespoons cilantro, chopped
¼ jalapeño pepper, seeded and minced
½ lime, squeezed
½ garlic clove, minced
Salt and pepper to taste

DIRECTIONS

GRILLED CHICKEN
In a medium bowl, whisk together olive oil, garlic, and dried herbs. Season generously with salt and pepper.

Add chicken to the bowl and toss to coat. Let marinate.

Preheat the grill to medium-high. Add chicken and grill until cooked through, about 6 minutes per side.

BROWN RICE & BLACK BEANS
In a large saucepan, sauté the onions in oil until tender.

Stir in the beans, tomatoes, 2 tablespoons of vinegar, garlic, salt, pepper, and cayenne. Bring to a boil.

Reduce heat. Simmer uncovered for 12-15 minutes or until desired consistency, stirring occasionally.

Add cooked brown rice and mix.

ASSEMBLE THE WRAP
Preheat the oven to 400°F.

Spread the chipotle sauce on the whole wheat wrap. Cut the chicken in strips and distribute equally in the middle of the wrap.

Add the black beans and brown rice mix.

Add the pico de gallo and top with jack cheese.

Roll up and let it toast in the oven for 10 minutes.

CARROT EXPRESS

MADLOVE RIBEYE STEAK

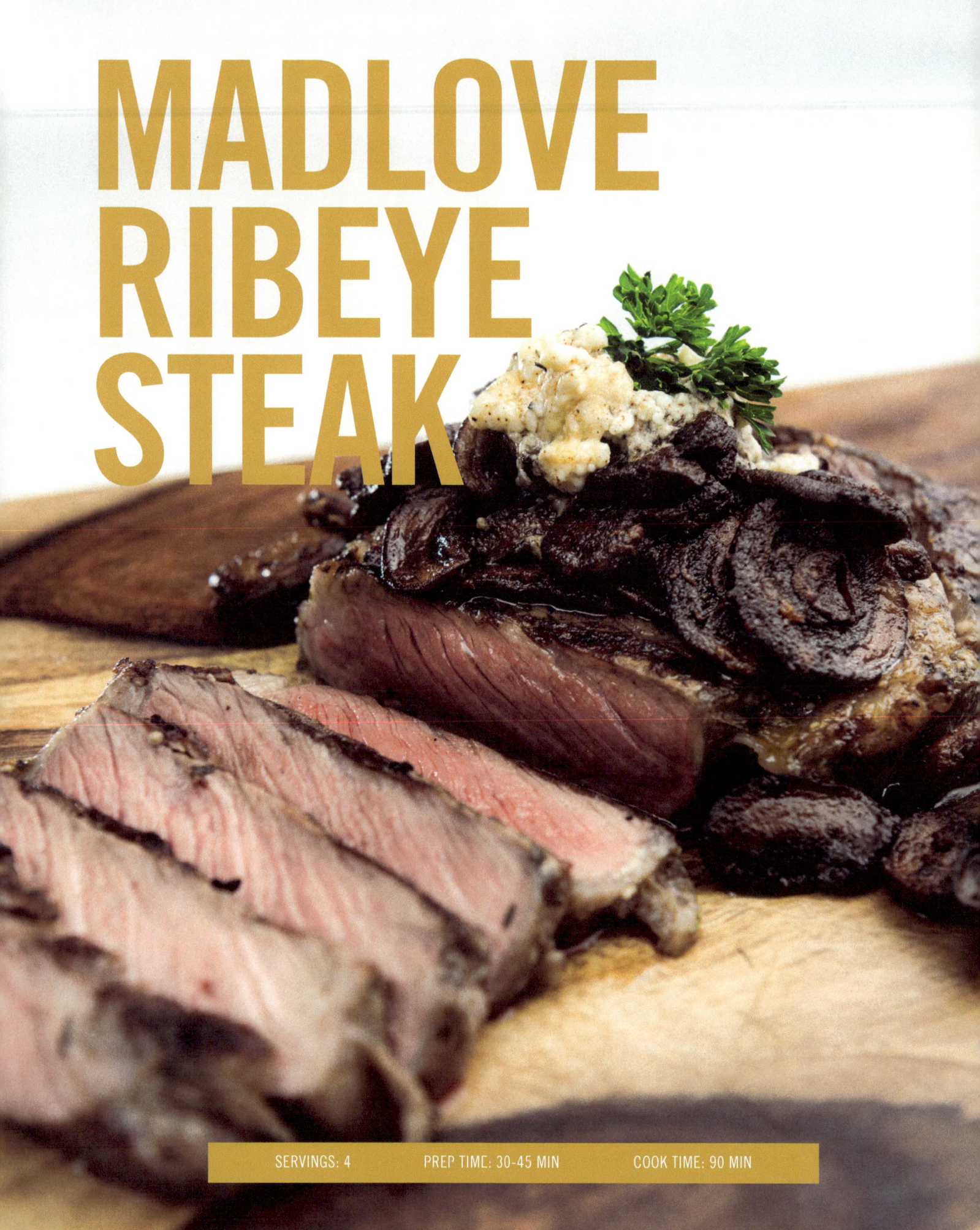

SERVINGS: 4   PREP TIME: 30-45 MIN   COOK TIME: 90 MIN

INGREDIENTS

18 ounces of boneless ribeye (1½-inch thick)
3 cups butter (or 6 sticks)
2 cups blue cheese
1 tablespoon salt
1 tablespoon black pepper
1 tablespoon thyme
1 tablespoon chili powder
1 tablespoon chipotle cinnamon
1 pound of small portobello mushrooms
1 bottle of Amarone wine

DIRECTIONS

STEAKS

Trim excess fat off steak, set aside, and bring to room temperature.

In a medium bowl add butter, blue cheese, salt, pepper, thyme, chili powder, chipotle cinnamon, and fold together with a spatula.

Set aside 1 cup of the butter mixture to be used for the mushrooms. Mushrooms should be washed and sliced into thirds.

Rub butter mixture over the steaks making sure to cover all areas.

Have a grill and large cast-iron skillet ready. This is where timing (which is the most important trick to master while cooking) is most important.
NOTE: Cast iron works best for these mushrooms, but any thick-walled pan will do just fine, warm it to medium.

Preheat your grill on medium-high and place steaks on the bottom rack.
NOTE: This will be a show since the fats from the butter will flare the fire up. Hold strong and do not touch the steak for 3 minutes.

Once the 3 minutes pass, rotate the steaks in a 90-degree angle on the same side for another 2 minutes to achieve grill marks.

Flip the steaks over and repeat the 3 and 2-minute rule. At this point, your steak will be a perfect medium rare. You can move steaks to the top rack of the grill or lower heat to medium-low, leaving steaks on the grill for another 4-6 minutes for a medium and medium-well done finish.

Once steaks have been removed, let them rest on a plate. Cover with aluminum foil.

MUSHROOMS

Heat cast-iron skillet to medium-high heat. Add remaining butter mixture and mushrooms to the pan. If your pan is not large enough, make in two batches, as mushrooms should be spread out in a single layer. Let them enjoy the butter braise and try not to move them too much.

Once caramelizing starts, add one glass of the Amarone to the mushrooms.
NOTE: It's ok, you just opened a bottle of Amarone and now have three glasses left to enjoy with your meal.

Stir until the butter and wine turn into a creamy state of perfection. Serve over each steak evenly and enjoy.

LATIN HOUSE GRILL

MAHI MAHI W. MANGO SALSA

SERVINGS: 1   PREP TIME: 15 MIN   COOK TIME: 10 MIN

INGREDIENTS

MAHI-MAHI
5-ounce mahi-mahi fillet
2 tablespoons extra virgin olive oil
Salt to taste
Pepper to taste

MANGO SALSA
1 mango, diced
½ red bell pepper, diced
1 lime, juiced
1 teaspoon extra virgin oil
Salt to taste
Pepper to taste
1 tablespoon cilantro, chopped
2 scallions for garnishing

KALE RAINBOW CHARD WITH GARLIC AND LEMON ZEST
1 bunch rainbow chard, trimmed and rinsed
1 bunch Tuscan kale
2 tablespoons extra virgin olive oil
1 garlic clove
½ lemon, juiced
1 pinch red pepper flakes

DIRECTIONS

MAHI-MAHI
Season and pan sear the mahi-mahi for about 6-7 minutes. Remove from the pan and let rest.

MANGO SALSA
In a bowl, combine all the ingredients and adjust the seasoning to taste.

Top the mahi-mahi fillet with the mango salsa.

KALE RAINBOW CHARD WITH GARLIC AND LEMON ZEST
Separate the stems of the chard from the leaves. Cut the leaves and thinly slice the stems.

Separate the leaves from the stems for the Tuscan kale. Roughly chop the leaves. Discard the stems.

Heat olive oil in a large skillet over medium heat. Stir in the chopped garlic, red pepper flakes, and chard stems. Cook for 3 minutes until the flavor of the garlic mellows and the stems begin to soften. Stir in the shredded chard leaves and Tuscan kale. Cook for 5 minutes over medium-low heat. Stir, cover, and continue cooking until the leaves are tender. Toss with lemon juice to serve.

CARILLON MIAMI

SERVINGS: 4   **PREP TIME:** 15 MIN   **COOK TIME:** 20 MIN

INGREDIENTS

4 cups quinoa, cooked
4 cups arugula
4 salmon fillets (5-6 ounces each)
2 avocados
1 cup cherry tomatoes, halved
1 cup fresh mango, diced
1 cup pickled cabbage (or fresh green cabbage)
1 lemon, cut in wedges
1 tablespoon sesame seeds

NOTE: If using fresh shaved green cabbage, we recommend tossing in olive oil, aged white wine vinegar, lemon juice, salt, and pepper.

DIRECTIONS

Preheat the oven to 425°F.

Season salmon filets with salt, pepper, and olive oil. Place on a baking sheet and bake for 15 minutes (or 10-12 mins if you prefer medium-rare).

ASSEMBLE BOWLS
Place arugula in a bowl and scoop cooked quinoa on top. Mix together.

Place salmon fillets in the center of the bowl.

Fan avocado and place off on a side of the bowl.

Add cherry tomatoes, mango, and cabbage.

Sprinkle a dash of sesame seeds over the bowl as a garnish.

Add lemon wedges on the side and serve with your favorite sauce, or pick up a bottle of Pura Vida Sauce for the true authentic taste.

NOTE: Alternatively, divide ingredients by 4 and prepare individual bowls for each guest following the same steps as above.

PURA VIDA

LOMO SALTADO

SERVINGS: 4   PREP TIME: 5 MIN   COOK TIME: 20 MIN

INGREDIENTS

4 NY strip steaks (14-16 ounces each)
1 red onion, cut in strips
2 plum tomatoes, cut in wedges
1 bunch scallions, chopped
2 tablespoons garlic, minced
¼ cup balsamic vinegar
4 tablespoons olive oil
1 tablespoon ground cumin
½ teaspoon salt
4 cups cooked white rice
1 pound frozen yuca fries

OPTIONAL
fresh cilantro for garnish

SALTADO SAUCE
½ cup soy sauce
½ cup oyster sauce
½ cup chicken stock

DIRECTIONS

Deep fry yuca fries for 4 minutes at 375°F (alternatively: Air fry for 15 minutes) or until golden brown. Set aside.

In a heavy bottom skillet over high heat, heat up olive oil.

Season steaks on both sides with salt and pepper.

Sear the steaks, cooking each one on both sides for 3-4 minutes depending on preference for doneness.

Remove steak from the pan and let rest.

Mix all ingredients for saltado sauce and set aside.

Using the same sear pan, add garlic, onions, cumin, and sauté for 3-4 minutes on medium heat.

Add tomatoes and scallions, continue to sauté for 3 more minutes.

Add balsamic vinegar and saltado sauce, simmer for 5 minutes.

Serve steak saltado atop yuca fries and white rice, garnish with fresh cilantro.

33 KITCHEN

PLANTAIN CRUSTED GROUPER

SERVINGS: 2   PREP TIME: 20 MIN   COOK TIME: 15 MIN

SPECIAL TOOLS: Immersion blender, food processor

INGREDIENTS

GUAVA SAUCE
1 8-ounce jar guava jelly
¼ cup orange juice (no pulp)
2 tablespoons fresh lime juice
¼ teaspoon coarse ground mustard
½ teaspoon cayenne pepper
½ teaspoon cardamom
¼ cup cilantro, finely chopped
Pinch of salt

GROUPER
2 6-ounce Florida grouper filets
3 eggs, beaten
½ cup flour
Salt and pepper to taste
1 cup unsalted mariquitas (plantain chips)

DIRECTIONS

GUAVA SAUCE
With an immersion blender add guava jelly, lime juice, orange juice, cayenne pepper, and cardamom. Blend gently. Avoid over blending as the mixture will thicken too much.

Once blended, add the coarse ground mustard, cilantro, and pinch of salt. Stir with a whisk. Cool overnight for better flavor.

GROUPER
Preheat your oven at 375°F and line an oiled baking sheet with parchment paper.

In a food processor, pulse the mariquitas (plantain chips) to a bread crumb texture.

Pat fish dry and season grouper with salt and pepper to taste.

In three separate bowls, add flour, beaten eggs, and mariquita crumbs.

Dredge fish in flour and then in egg. Lastly, cover only the top of the fish in mariquita crumbs.

Place fish on the baking sheet and bake for 20-22 minutes.

TO ASSEMBLE
Warm up the guava sauce in a saucepan until it becomes a smooth glaze-like texture.

Serve plantain crusted grouper over jasmine rice and grilled asparagus or your favorite starch and veggies.

CHEFS ON THE RUN

RABO ENCENDIDO

SERVINGS: 4　　PREP TIME: 15 MIN　　COOK TIME: 3 HRS

INGREDIENTS

4 pounds oxtail
1 medium Spanish onion, peeled and chopped into medium-size pieces
1 green bell pepper, seeded and chopped into small pieces
1 red bell pepper, seeded and chopped into small pieces
1 medium-size carrot, peeled and diced
2 cups of tomato paste
3 tablespoons garlic, minced
½ teaspoon allspice
½ teaspoon cumin
4 bay leaves
2 cups of beef stock
1 cup of red cooking wine
Olive oil
Salt to taste
Pepper to taste

DIRECTIONS

Trim some of the fat if it is too fatty. Season oxtail with salt and pepper, covering all sides.

In a large pot, bring olive oil to high heat, and sear oxtail until brown on all sides.

Set oxtail aside and in the same pot, sauté garlic, onion, peppers, and carrots until tender.

Place oxtails in a pot and add tomato paste, beef stock, and wine.

Bring to a simmer and add cumin, allspice, and bay leaves.

Cover with aluminum foil and place in the oven at 325°F for 2-2.5 hours. Oxtails should be tender.

Salt and pepper to taste.

FINKA TABLE & TAP

REVERSE-SEARED RACK OF LAMB

SERVINGS: 2 PREP TIME: 15 MIN COOK TIME: 45 MIN

SPECIAL TOOLS: Food processor, roasting rack

INGREDIENTS

1½ pounds lamb
1 stick butter
1 tablespoon garlic
1 tablespoon roasted red pepper
1 tablespoon white onion
½ tablespoon thyme
½ tablespoon oregano
1 tablespoon kosher salt
¼ teaspoon paprika
Juice of ½ lemon

DIRECTIONS

Leave the butter out for approximately 1-2 hours until softened (not melted). Blend with all ingredients in the food processor on low for 30 seconds.

Preheat the oven to 400°F.

Pat lamb rack dry with a paper towel.

Sprinkle salt and pepper to taste over the rack.

Rub butter generously around lamb and place on a roasting rack in the oven for 25 minutes.

Remove rack from the oven and using tongs, transfer rack over to a very hot cast-iron skillet. Place the lamb arched side down and allow to sear.

Rest on a cutting board for 5 minutes. Slice and enjoy.

GET REAL

SERVINGS: 4   PREP TIME: 15 MIN   COOK TIME: 10 MIN

INGREDIENTS

1 pound dry spaghetti
6 ounces pork guanciale, small diced
1 cup grana padano parmesan cheese, grated
8 egg yolks
Kosher salt to taste
Black pepper to taste
Parmigiano-reggiano to taste

DIRECTIONS

Bring 6-quarts of salted water to a boil.

Add pasta and cook, stirring occasionally.

In a mixing bowl, whisk together the eggs yolk and the grana padano parmesan cheese.

Add a pinch of salt and generous amount of black pepper.

Also heat a large pan, add the pork guanciale, and sauté until the fat gets crispy. Remove from heat and set aside.

About 2 minutes before it ends, when the pasta is "al dente", drain and reserve 3 cups of pasta cooking water.

Add the pasta to the pan with the pork and stir for about 1 minute.

Stir in cheese mixture, adding some pasta water for creaminess or if the pasta is too dry.

Divide the pasta in 4 pasta bowls, add some parmesan cheese, and top with black pepper.

LUNA PARK

SPECIAL TOOLS: Food processor

INGREDIENTS

1 package of naan flatbread (or flatbread of choice)
1 package of top round steak, pounded thin (approximately 4 steaks)
½ cup Creamy Mango Sauce
1 small sweet onion
1 green bell pepper
1 red bell pepper
½ cup button mushrooms
1 cup shredded melty cheese of choice (we like gruyère)
Sweet and spicy hot sauce
Olive oil
Salt and pepper to taste
½ cup arugula

CREAMY MANGO SAUCE
1 cup pureed fresh mango
¼ cup greek yogurt
1 tablespoon sweet and spicy hot sauce

DIRECTIONS

CREAMY MANGO SAUCE
Puree fresh mango in the food processor until smooth. Add yogurt and hot sauce until well blended. Adjust spice to taste and refrigerate. Mango sauce can be made a day ahead.

PHILLY FLATBREAD
Pound steaks thinly and season lightly with salt and pepper. Marinate overnight or for at least two hours.

Slice all veggies to about a ⅛-inch thickness. Season with salt and pepper, and sauté at medium-high heat for 1-2 minutes. Veggies should be crisp and not soggy. Push all veggies to one side of the pan and add steak. Cook for 1-2 minutes on each side until the steak starts to brown. Do not overcook.

Slice steak against the grain to about ¼-inch thick, and mix with veggies.

Brush 2 naan flatbreads with olive oil.

Spread steak and veggie mixture evenly between the two flatbreads. Sprinkle it with cheese.

Place directly on the center rack in a preheated oven 400°F for 6-7 minutes, or until the cheese is melted. Remove from the oven.

Add sweet & spicy hot sauce according to your heat index.
Top flatbread with peppery arugula, and drizzle creamy mango sauce.

MIAMI GRILL

TACOS DE LENGUA

YIELDS: 20 TACOS | PREP TIME: 10 MIN | COOK TIME: 75 MIN

SPECIAL TOOLS: Pressure cooker, blow torch or gas burner

INGREDIENTS

2 beef tongues, whole and thawed
2 white onions, whole
4 bay leaves
1 12-ounce bottle of Victoria Lager
Salt to taste
3 cups water
Corn tortillas
Fresh cilantro leaves, chopped
½ white onion, diced
1 lime, quartered

DIRECTIONS

Pour water and beer into the pressure cooker.

Cut onions in half. Hold the onion with tongs and carefully char the inside and outside of the onion with a torch until black.

Using tongs, carefully toast the bay leaves as well.

Place charred onions on the base of the pressure cooker.
NOTE: If you don't have a pressure cooker, follow all of the same procedures stated above but instead place ingredients in an oven-safe dish and braise in the oven until tender, about 4 hours at 350°F.

Continue to add the tongues, bay leaves, and salt.

Place the pressure cooker on a stove set to high heat. Lock the lid and set the pressure to "High" (or 15psi).

Once the pressure cooker reaches 15psi, lower the heat, and continue to cook for 75 minutes.

Let the pressure cooker depressurize naturally or place under running water to depressurize quicker.

Remove tongues from the pot and put aside until cool enough to handle. Keep everything else in the pot.

The skin on the tongue should peel away easily. Discard skin and dice into bite-sized cubes.

Blend the remaining liquid and cooked onions until smooth.

Combine the jus from the blender with the diced tongue. Warm together in a pot, or better yet, sear on a hot pan with a little oil.

Nothing left to do but to bring out your best corn tortillas and start assembling tacos and topping with fresh cilantro, white onion, and a squeeze of lime.

TAQUIZA

SERVINGS: 4-6   PREP TIME: 30 MIN   COOK TIME: 15 MIN

INGREDIENTS

2 pounds flank steak, cut into 4 pieces
1 green bell pepper, cored and quartered
2 large onions, cut in half
2 tablespoons of complete seasoning
1 cup mojo marinade, diluted with 1 cup of water

DIRECTIONS

In a large saucepan, combine the flank steak with the bell pepper, onions, and complete seasoning. Add enough water to cover and bring to a boil. Simmer over medium heat for 20 minutes.

Transfer the flank steak to a work surface and let the steak cool. Shred the meat and transfer it to a bowl.

Heat a large flat griddle on high until very hot. Working in batches, spread the shredded beef on the griddle in a thin layer and season with complete seasoning.

Cook over high heat, turning once or twice, until sizzling and crispy in spots. Drizzle with mojo marinade, about 6 minutes per batch. Transfer to a platter and serve.

CUBAN GUYS

LITERALL

Y, SWEET

ADELA'S FLAN

SERVINGS: 12 PREP TIME: 25 MIN COOK TIME: 60 MIN

SPECIAL TOOLS: Electric mixer, flan mold

INGREDIENTS

1 cup sugar
5 eggs
2 14-ounce cans sweetened condensed milk
2 12-ounce cans evaporated milk
1 tablespoon vanilla extract
3 tablespoons dark rum
2 tablespoons cornstarch, dissolved in 1 tablespoon of water

OPTIONAL
Shaved dark/white chocolate
Peaches
Strawberries
Cherries
Toasted coconut flakes

DIRECTIONS

Preheat the oven to 350°F degrees.

In a medium-sized saucepan over medium-low heat, melt ½ cup sugar until liquified and golden in color, about 15 minutes. Carefully pour hot syrup onto a 9-inch round glass baking dish or flan mold, turning the dish to evenly coat the bottom and sides. Set aside.

In a large bowl, mix eggs, condensed milk, evaporated milk, vanilla, rum, and the remaining sugar with an electric mixer until smooth. Add the dissolved cornstarch and mix. Pour egg mixture onto caramelized sugar flan mold.

Place the flan mold onto a larger baking pan and pour water into the pan to reach a depth of an inch. Bake for 50-60 minutes or until the center is set.

Remove flan mold from the baking dish and let cool for 1 hour. Refrigerate overnight.

To unmold, run a thin rubber spatula around the edges of the flan and then invert onto a plate.

Garnish with shaved dark/white chocolate, peaches, strawberries, cherries, and toasted coconut flakes.

CHEF CHRIS VALDES

CAP'N CRUNCH PANCAKES

SERVINGS: 4 PREP TIME: 10 MIN COOK TIME: 10-15 MIN

INGREDIENTS

VANILLA BUTTER
1 stick unsalted butter, room temperature
½ teaspoon vanilla bean or 1 teaspoon vanilla extract
¼ teaspoon kosher salt

PANCAKES
½ cup Cap'n Crunch cereal, plus more to finish
1 cup plus 2 tablespoons all-purpose flour
1½ tablespoons granulated sugar
1 teaspoon kosher salt
1 tablespoon baking powder
1¼ cups whole milk
2 large eggs, lightly whisked
6 tablespoons melted unsalted butter, plus more for the skillet

CONDENSED MILK SYRUP
1 cup condensed milk
¼ cup heavy cream
Pinch of kosher salt

DIRECTIONS

VANILLA BUTTER
In a medium bowl, mix together the butter and vanilla until well combined.

Refrigerate while making the pancakes.

PANCAKES
In a food processor, add the cereal and pulse until it is ground to a fine powder. Transfer to a medium bowl and add the flour, sugar, salt, and baking powder.

In a separate bowl, whisk together the milk, eggs, and melted butter. Mix the wet ingredients into the dry ingredients just until combined.

Set a griddle or large nonstick skillet over medium-high heat. Grease lightly with a bit of melted butter and add ¼ cup spoonful of batter to the pan, making sure to space the pancakes at least 2 inches apart. Once bubbles begin to form on the top of the pancakes, after 4-5 minutes, carefully flip them and cook until the second side is golden brown, 1-2 minutes. Repeat with the remaining batter until it is all used.

CONDENSED-MILK SYRUP
In a medium bowl, whisk together the condensed milk, heavy cream, and salt.

Serve the pancakes with the vanilla butter and condensed-milk syrup. Top with extra Cap'n Crunch cereal.

EATING HOUSE

CHOCOLATE GANACHE DOUGHNUT

YIELDS: 15 PIECES   PREP TIME: 15 MIN   COOK TIME: 45 MIN

SPECIAL TOOLS: Doughnut mold

INGREDIENTS

DOUGHNUTS
3 cups flour
1½ cups sunflower oil
1 cup cacao powder
1½ cups buttermilk
2 teaspoons baking soda
2 teaspoons vanilla extract
½ teaspoon salt
2½ cups white sugar
3 eggs

GANACHE
½ cup heavy cream
8 ounces of semi-sweet chocolate

DIRECTIONS

DOUGHNUTS
Preheat your oven to 350°F.

Grease doughnut molds and place parchment paper in the bottom of each one on top of a tray.

In a bowl, add the flour together with the baking soda and cocoa until well combined, and set aside.

In another bowl, mix the eggs together with the buttermilk, sunflower oil, and vanilla extract.

Split the dry ingredients into two and add one batch at a time to the wet ingredients until everything is combined and smooth.

Add the sugar to the rest of the mixture and mix until it is well incorporated.

Place the mixture into the molds and bake for 25 minutes. Bake until a knife comes out clean when inserting it.

Let the doughnuts cool for 10 minutes in their molds. Then, trim any excess doughnut from the molds and pass a knife around the edges of the mold to loosen.

Flip the doughnuts onto a rack to cool completely.

GANACHE
Heat your heavy cream on a stovetop or in the microwave and bring it to a boil.

Place your chocolate in a bowl. Add the heavy cream into the chocolate bowl, and whisk the mixture until well combined.

Set aside your ganache for 5 minutes.

Pour the desired amount of chocolate ganache over the doughnuts.

HONEYBEE DOUGHNUTS

COCONUT ARROZ CON LECHE

SERVINGS: 8   PREP TIME: 15 MIN   COOK TIME: 90 MIN

SPECIAL TOOL: ZESTER

INGREDIENTS

- 1 14-ounce package Valencia short-grain rice
- 6¼ cups water
- 2 cinnamon sticks
- 1 large lime, zested
- ¼ teaspoon salt
- 2 cups whole milk
- 2 14-ounce cans condensed milk
- 1 13.5-ounce can unsweetened coconut milk
- 1 15-ounce can cream of coconut
- 1¾ cups granulated sugar
- 2 teaspoons pure vanilla extract
- 2 teaspoons coconut extract
- 1 cup sweetened coconut flakes
- Cinnamon powder for garnish

OPTIONAL
- 1 more cup sweetened coconut flakes

DIRECTIONS

In a medium-sized bowl, pour in the whole bag of Valencia rice. Fill the bowl with water until rice is completely covered. Leave rice soaking overnight.

Once the rice has soaked overnight, drain the rice and place rice inside a large pot. Add 6¼ cups of water to the pot, along with cinnamon sticks and ¼ teaspoon of salt. Zest the whole lime and add the zest to the pot and stir.

Place the pot on the stove over medium-high heat and cover. Do not leave unattended as it will boil quickly. Once the water begins to boil, stir the rice well, cover the pot again and turn the heat down to a low-medium setting, allowing for water to come to a simmer but not boil. Let it cook covered in a low simmer for 30 minutes.
NOTE: Do not be afraid if after the 30 minutes you see that not all the water has evaporated, that's okay.

While rice is simmering, open all your cans of condensed milk, coconut milk, and cream of coconut. Measure out the 2 cups of whole milk. Uncover the pot and start to pour in all your milk, stirring after each of the milks have been incorporated.

Measure out the pure vanilla extract and add to the pot. Do the same with the coconut extract.

Take the one cup of sweetened coconut flakes and add it in. Make sure to stir everything together. At this point, you should take a spoon and taste it. You may add more sugar if you desire more sweetness.

Leave the pot uncovered for the rest of the hour. Put the heat up a bit, just enough to bring it to a simmer.
NOTE: The secret for a creamy arroz con leche is to keep stirring constantly as you would a risotto.

Once you've reached the cooking time and you feel it's at the consistency you desire, transfer the coconut arroz con leche into a large food container or in several medium-sized containers. You can decide to divide them into individual portions or to keep them in the food containers. Leave uncovered to cool for 1 hour, then cover and place in the refrigerator.

Refrigerate for at least 4 hours before serving. When serving, sprinkle each portion with cinnamon powder.

OPTIONAL
Preheat the oven to 350°F. Lay out the remaining cup of sweetened coconut flakes evenly onto a cookie sheet and toast in the oven until they turn light brown. Make sure you are watching it as the coconut will burn quickly because of the sugar.

Take out the cookie sheet and let the toasted coconut flakes cool completely. You may then store them in a zippered plastic bag, so they stay fresh and crispy.

Garnish each portion with this toasted coconut for some added texture and coconut flavor.

LATIN AMERICAN BAKERY & CAFE

CRÈME BRÛLÉE PIE

| SERVINGS: 12 | PREP TIME: 1 HR | COOK TIME: 2 HRS | SPECIAL TOOLS: STAND MIXER |

INGREDIENTS

SWEET PASTRY CRUST
2 cups all-purpose flour, plus more as needed
¼ teaspoon salt
¼ cup sugar
½ cup cold butter, cut into 8 pieces
2 large eggs
Water (as needed)

CRÈME BRÛLÉE MIX
4 cups heavy cream
¾ cup sugar
10 large egg yolks
¾ teaspoon pure vanilla extract

RASPBERRY SAUCE
1½ cups defrosted frozen raspberries or fresh raspberries
3 tablespoons superfine sugar
1 teaspoon fresh lemon juice

GARNISH AND ASSEMBLE
3 cups fresh seasonal berries
⅓ cup light brown granulated sugar

DIRECTIONS

CRUST
In a food processor fitted with the metal blade, process 2 cups of flour, salt, and sugar briefly to mix. Add the butter and process just until very coarse crumbs form.

Drop in the eggs through the feed tube and process just until the dough begins to form into a solid mass. Do not over process. The dough should be soft but not dry or sticky. If too soft, add a tablespoon more flour; if too dry, add a teaspoon of water. Gather the dough into a disk, wrap well, and refrigerate for about 30 minutes.

Preheat the oven to 375°F. On a lightly floured surface, roll the dough into a circle that is 14 inches in diameter. Carefully drape into a 9-inch springform pan, pressing against the bottom and about 1¾-inch up the side. If the dough tears, just press together. Prick the bottom and side of the crust liberally with a fork.

Line the crust with aluminum foil and fill with dry beans to keep the crust from shrinking as it bakes. Bake in the center of the oven for about 15 minutes. Remove the foil and beans and continue baking another 10 to 12 minutes or until lightly browned. Remove to a wire rack and cool completely before filling. Can be made a day ahead.

CRÈME BRÛLÉE
Preheat the oven to 325°F. Lightly grease a 2½-quart baking dish.

In a heavy saucepan, heat the cream over medium heat just until bubbles appear around the edge.

Meanwhile, in a large bowl, whisk the sugar, egg yolks, and vanilla until well combined. Still whisking briskly, very slowly add the hot cream in a steady stream. Pour this custard through a sieve into the prepared baking dish and stand the dish in a larger pan of warm water.

Bake the custard 30 to 35 minutes or until completely set but still slightly jiggly in the center.
Remove to a wire rack and let cool. Cover and refrigerate overnight.

RASPBERRY SAUCE
In a food processor fitted with the metal blade, process all the ingredients together. Pass through a strainer, discarding the seeds.

TO ASSEMBLE
Spoon about a third of the crème brûlée mix into the bottom of the crust. Strew half the berries over, then layer half the remaining crème brûlée mix and the remaining berries. End with the remaining mix. Cover lightly and refrigerate several hours or overnight.

About 60-90 minutes before serving, preheat the broiler. Use a sieve to distribute the granulated sugar evenly over the top. If necessary, cover any exposed crust edges with foil. Place the pie 4-5 inches from the broiler heat and broil 1-2 minutes or until the sugar melts and bubbles. Watch carefully as it burns quickly. Alternatively, you can use a kitchen torch to brown the sugar.

Remove and cool, then refrigerate until serving time. Remove the side of the pan before cutting. The sugar will get crackly. When serving, punch it with the point of a sharp knife to break it, if necessary. Drizzle about a generous tablespoon of the raspberry sauce around or beside each serving.

MAX'S GRILLE

SPECIAL TOOLS: Pie Pan

INGREDIENTS

12 ounces egg yolks
3 cups sweetened condensed milk
3 cups fresh-squeezed lime juice
¾ ounce corn starch

PIE CRUST
2 cups graham cracker crumbs
1 tablespoon cinnamon powder
½ cup melted butter
2 tablespoons sugar

DIRECTIONS

Preheat the oven to 350°F.

In a small bowl, combine graham cracker crumbs, cinnamon powder, sugar, and melted butter.
Mix well and spread evenly over the pie tin pressing firmly to set the crust then place it aside.

In a medium bowl, combine condensed milk, lime juice, egg yolks, and cornstarch.
Mix well and pour into graham cracker crust.

Bake in a preheated oven for 25-30 minutes until tiny pinholes bubbles burst on the surface of the pie.
Be careful to not brown the pie.

Chill pie in the refrigerator for 50 minutes before serving. Garnish with a sliced lime wedge and whipped cream.

MONTY'S RAW BAR

PASTELITOS DE GUAYABA Y QUESO

YIELDS: 4-6 PIECES   PREP TIME: 30 MIN   COOK TIME: 15-20 MIN

INGREDIENTS

One box of puff pastry (2 sheets), thawed
2 ounces guayaba
2 ounces cream cheese
1 egg beaten
Almíbar

GUAYABA
2 ounces instant corn starch
1½ cups sugar
2 cups natural guava pulp
1 cup water
Red food coloring

ALMÍBAR
4 cups sugar
2 cups water
¾ cups corn syrup

DIRECTIONS

GUAYABA
Combine instant corn starch and sugar into a mixer. Add guava pulp and mix on medium-low for 5 minutes.

Use a rubber spatula to scrape the sides and bottom of the bowl.

Add water and mix on medium-low for another 5 minutes. Add one drop of red food coloring and mix for another 2 minutes at the same speed.

Transfer mixture into a piping bag or zippered plastic bag with a nickel-sized corner cut off.

ALMÍBAR
Boil sugar and water over medium heat until the sugar dissolves.

Remove from heat and pour it into a mixer. Add corn syrup and mix on low speed for 15 minutes.

PASTELITOS
Preheat the oven to 400°F.

Remove puff pastry from packaging and use the folded lines to cut each sheet into equal square-shaped slices. Set aside one sheet (half of the squares).

Squeeze a dollop of homemade guayaba in the center of half the slices of puff pastry. Add a small scoop of cream cheese directly on top of the guayaba.

Top each square with the reserved pieces of puff pastry. Do not flatten or press the edges together.

Brush the top of each pastry with egg wash. Make a small cut on the top of each pastry to allow heat to vent.

Place on a baking sheet and bake until golden, about 15 to 20 minutes. While pastelitos are baking, make your almíbar.

Remove from the oven and immediately brush the top of each with a generous amount of almíbar.

Allow to cool and enjoy.

CAO BAKERY

HOY S

BEBE

SPECIAL THANKS TO
GABE URRUTIA

My love affair with Miami started in the 4th grade. I was tasked with writing a report about the city I grew up in. This was way before the internet became popular, I didn't have Google or Siri, so I turned to the original search engine: my parents.

My parents migrated from Cuba and Chile. Their cultures and traditions influenced so many different experiences growing up. My Cuban side taught me the art of making cafecito, how to make batidos de trigo & mamey, and guarapo was commonplace for a refreshing pick-me-up. My Chilean side introduced me to the lesser-known but equally delicious mote con huesillo, cola de mono, and even piscola.

While they were telling me all about Miami's history, my dad used a word that really stuck out — Cosmopolitan. He explained it to me as a cocktail of cultures.

Years later, as I was working on Miami's first cocktail book, I found out the Cosmopolitan cocktail has a history in Miami. Made popular on a famous TV show about four women in New York City, the Cosmo was actually invented at The Strand in Miami Beach by the wonderful Cheryl Cook. A rep gave her a bottle of vodka and the rest is history. At least that's our story.

Still, there is nothing truer than how my Dad defined this city, and how Cheryl named that cocktail. Miami is a worldly cocktail of cultures that when mixed, makes the perfect drink. Today, Miami is home to some of the best bars and restaurants in the world, and I am so lucky to be a part of its history. Enjoy this book with some recipes you have enjoyed at restaurants throughout the years while pairing it with some cocktails I created for the occasion.

Miami is my first love, my home, and one of the best places to drink and eat on earth.

Gabe Urrutia

CALLE OCHO MOJITO

INGREDIENTS

2 ounces white rum
1 ounce Redland guava marmalade
.75 ounce lime juice
.5 ounce vanilla bean syrup
5 mint leaves
1 dash Angostura Bitters
Top with soda water

DIRECTIONS

Add all ingredients except soda water to a shaker.

Shake until chilled.

Strain over fresh ice into highball glass.

Garnish with lime wheel and mint sprig.

NOTE: Redland Guava Marmalade is locally sourced from PG Tropicals in Homestead. If you're not in Miami, look for guava marmalade in your local supermarket.

To make your own VANILLA BEAN SYRUP
One cup water to one cup granulated sugar to a saucepan on medium heat. Slice one vanilla pod (the long way) and add the seeds, as well as the whole pod to the pan. Stir until sugar is dissolved and let sit over heat for 5 minutes. Turn off heat and let sit for another 20 minutes. Add syrup to a storage container, label, and store in the refrigerator.

GABE URRUTIA

INGREDIENTS

1.5 ounces of Coconut Cartel Special Añejo Rum
3.5 ounces of Guatemalan espresso
.5 ounce of simple syrup

OPTIONAL
Whipping cream or alternative non-dairy milk

NOTE: Coconut Cartel Rum is available on coconutcartel.co

DIRECTIONS

Brew two shots of espresso. Let chill to room temperature.

In a shaker combine espresso, simple syrup, rum, and ice.

Shake vigorously for 20-30 seconds. Strain into coup glass.

Garnish with freshly ground Guatemalan coffee beans.

OPTIONAL
Make it creamy by adding 1-2 barspoons of whipping cream or a splash of your favorite alternative non-dairy milk.

COCONUT CARTEL

LA VECINA MARGARITA

INGREDIENTS

2 ounces blanco tequila
1.5 ounce mango puree
.5 ounce jalapeño-infused simple syrup
.75 ounce lime juice
Tajín

DIRECTIONS

Add all ingredients to shaker over ice and shake until chilled.

Strain over fresh ice in rocks glass.

Garnish with Tajín rim and lime wedge.

To make your own JALAPEÑO-INFUSED SYRUP
Add 1 cup water to 1 cup sugar in a saucepan over medium heat, and add 1 jalapeño pepper sliced. Stir until sugar is dissolved in water. Reduce to low heat. Let sit for 10 minutes. Turn heat off and let sit for another 10 minutes. Strain into container and label with date.

To make your own MANGO PUREE
Add 1 cup sugar and 1 cup water to saucepan over medium heat until sugar is dissolved. Set aside. Peel 4 mangos and remove seeds. Add mangos, zest of 1 lime, simple syrup, 1 ounce fresh lime juice into blender. Blend until smooth. Strain over a fine mesh strainer 3 times. Add puree to a container and label with date.

GABE URRUTIA

SAGUESERA OLD FASHIONED

INGREDIENTS

2 ounces aged rum
.5 ounce Toasted Key Lime-Coconut Syrup
    1 cup water
    1 cup sugar
    1 cup shredded coconut
    Zest of 4 key limes
2 dashes Angostura Bitters
Garnish with orange peel and key lime zest

DIRECTIONS

Stir all ingredients in mixing glass except orange peel.

Pour cocktail in rocks glass over coconut water cube.

Express orange peel oil over cocktail and dispose of peel.

To make your own COCONUT WATER ICE CUBES
Use silicone ice molds to make large coconut water cubes.

To make your own TOASTED KEY LIME-COCONUT SYRUP
1 cup water, 1 cup sugar, 1 cup shredded coconut, zest of 4 key limes. First toast coconut on low until lightly toasted. Add water and sugar to the saucepan on medium heat with the shredded coconut and key lime zest. Add syrup to container, label with date, and store in the refrigerator.

GABE URRUTIA

INGREDIENTS

PIÑA COLADA
1 ounce white rum
.5 ounce aged rum
.75 ounce cream of coconut
.5 ounce pineapple juice
.5 ounce lime juice
1 ounce Cuban espresso

STRAWBERRY DAIQUIRI
1 ounce spiced rum
.5 ounce white rum
1 ounce strawberry puree
.5 ounce demerara syrup
.5 ounce lime juice

DIRECTIONS

Each recipe is created separately.

STRAWBERRY DAIQUIRI
Add ingredients into shaker and shake until chilled.

PIÑA COLADA
Add ingredients into shaker and shake until chilled.

In a Hurricane glass, add piña colada to bottom of the glass.

Add crushed ice to the top.

Layer strawberry daiquiri over crushed iced carefully.

Add more crushed ice on top. Garnish with pineapple leaf.

To make your own DEMERARA SYRUP
1 cup demerara sugar to 1 cup water. Add to a saucepan over medium heat until sugar is dissolved into water. Set aside to cool. Label and store in the refrigerator.

To make your own STRAWBERRY PUREE
Add ½ cup sugar to ½ cup water, add to a medium saucepan, set aside. Wash and hull 1 pound of fresh strawberries. Add syrup and strawberries to blender. Blend until smooth. Strain, label, and store in the refrigerator.

GABE URRUTIA

TROPICAL CAIPIRINHA

INGREDIENTS

1.5 ounces caçhaca
.75 ounce passion fruit liqueur
.75 ounce grilled pineapple-honey syrup
.75 ounce lime juice
Top with your favorite Lager

DIRECTIONS

Add all ingredients except garnish and beer to shaker over ice.

Shake until chilled.

Strain over fresh ice into rocks glass.

Garnish with grilled pineapple wedge.

To make your own GRILLED PINEAPPLE-HONEY SYRUP
Grill pineapple slices over charcoal or wood for 2 minutes on each side. Set aside a grilled pineapple wedge for garnish. Cut pineapples to fit into blender. Turn into puree. Strain over fine mesh strainer. Add 1 cup pineapple juice to 1 cup honey on low heat. Stir until fully dissolved.

GABE URRUTIA

WE LOV
MIAMI

E YOU,

THE RECIPES

SMALL BITES, BRO

18	Berry Hemp Banana Acai Bowl
20	Chorizo Croqueta
22	Conch Fritters
24	Elote
26	Grilled Shrimp & Avocado Tartine
28	Heart of Palm Ceviche
30	Mixed Seafood Ceviche
32	Parmesan Brussels Sprouts w. Chimichurri
34	Reuben Croqueta
36	Shrimp Gyoza
38	Snapper Ceviche
40	Spicy Tuna Salad
42	Sunday Brunch Croqueta

HAY HAMBRE

46	Abuela's Ham & Chorizo Cuban Macaroni
48	BEAST-loaf
50	Big Beef Ribs
52	Blackened Fish Tacos
54	Chicken Cacciatore
56	Chimichurri Steak Tacos
58	Enchiladas de Mariscos
60	Gnocchi Al Pesto
62	Guava BBQ Ribs
64	Green Curried Mussels
66	Homemade Cuban Frita Burger
68	Jupiña Express
70	Legal Wrap
72	Madlove Ribeye Steak
74	Mahi Mahi w. Mango Salsa
76	Mango Salmon Bowl
78	Lomo Saltado
80	Plantain Crusted Grouper
82	Rabo Encendido
84	Reverse-Seared Rack of Lamb
86	Spaghetti Carbonara
88	Spicy Mango Philly Cheesesteak Flatbread
90	Tacos de Lengua
92	Vaca Frita

LITERALLY, SWEET

96	Adela's Flan
98	Cap'n Crunch Pancakes
100	Chocolate Ganache Doughnut
102	Coconut Arroz con Leche
104	Crème Brûlée Pie
106	Key Lime Pie
108	Pastelitos de Guayaba y Queso

HOY SE BEBE

114	Calle Ocho Mojito
116	Cartel Carajillo
118	La Vecina Margarita
120	Saguesera Old Fashioned
122	Miami's Vice
124	Tropical Caipirinha

CREDITS

Creative Direction by Jonathan Morffi
Photography by Michael Geronazzo
Production by Brandon Rodriguez
Project Management by Maite Figueroa
Copy Editing by Michael Campos
Proofreading by Dina Allende

Financial Sponsor
MAHMUD SHIHADEH, DOWNSTAIRS

Location Sponsors
TRP TASTE
THE RITZ-CARLTON RESIDENCES, SUNNY ISLES BEACH

Media Sponsor
YELP MIAMI

Equipment Sponsor
T-REX CREATIVE

Restaurant Outreach
DINA ALLENDE, CLIQUE PR

Talent Sponsors
STELLAR TALENT AGENCY
YANA RYBINA
MICHELLE GUERRA

Legal Sponsor
PERERA BARNHART ALEMÁN, ATTORNEYS AT LAW

Wardrobe Sponsor
COS STORES, AVENTURA MALL

ALEXANDER QUAN
for donating @tasteofmiami

www.ingramcontent.com/pod-product-compliance
Lightning Source LLC
Chambersburg PA
CBHW041716160426
43209CB00018B/1848